Home is Where the Heart Is

Address & Phone Book

By

Linda Blair

ISBN: 1-4107-3361-0 (e-book)
ISBN: 1-4107-4523-6 (Paperback)

This book is printed on acid free paper.

1st Books - rev. 09/19/03

A

Always be friendly

Special notes to remember ......

_____
_____
_____
_____
_____
_____
_____
_____
_____
_____
_____
_____
_____
_____
_____
_____
_____
_____

Name _____

Address _____

City, State, Zip Code _____

Phone Nu. _____ Email _____

Name _____

Address _____

City, State, Zip Code _____

Phone Nu. _____ Email _____

Name _____

Address _____

City, State, Zip Code _____

Phone Nu. _____ Email _____

Name _____

Address _____

City, State, Zip Code _____

Phone Nu. _____ Email _____

Name _____

Address _____

City, State, Zip Code _____

Phone Nu. _____ Email _____

Name _____

Address _____

City, State, Zip Code _____

Phone Nu. _____ Email _____

Name _____

Address _____

City, State, Zip Code _____

Phone Nu. _____ Email _____

Name _____

Address _____

City, State, Zip Code _____

Phone Nu. _____ Email _____

Name _____

Address _____

City, State, Zip Code _____

Phone Nu. _____ Email _____

Name _____

Address _____

City, State, Zip Code _____

Phone Nu. _____ Email _____

Name _____

Address _____

City, State, Zip Code _____

Phone Nu. _____ Email _____

Name _____

Address _____

City, State, Zip Code _____

Phone Nu. _____ Email _____

Name _____
Address _____
City, State, Zip Code _____
Phone Nu. _____ Email _____

Name _____
Address _____
City, State, Zip Code _____
Phone Nu. _____ Email _____

Name _____
Address _____
City, State, Zip Code _____
Phone Nu. _____ Email _____

Name _____
Address _____
City, State, Zip Code _____
Phone Nu. _____ Email _____

B

Believe in friends

Special notes to remember ......

_____
_____
_____
_____
_____
_____
_____
_____
_____
_____
_____
_____
_____
_____
_____
_____
_____

Name _____

Address _____

City, State, Zip Code _____

Phone Nu. _____ Email _____

Name _____

Address _____

City, State, Zip Code _____

Phone Nu. _____ Email _____

Name _____

Address _____

City, State, Zip Code _____

Phone Nu. _____ Email _____

Name _____

Address _____

City, State, Zip Code _____

Phone Nu. _____ Email _____

Name _____

Address _____

City, State, Zip Code _____

Phone Nu. _____ Email _____

Name _____

Address _____

City, State, Zip Code _____

Phone Nu. _____ Email _____

Name _____

Address _____

City, State, Zip Code _____

Phone Nu. _____ Email _____

Name _____

Address _____

City, State, Zip Code _____

Phone Nu. _____ Email _____

Name _____

Address _____

City, State, Zip Code _____

Phone Nu. _____ Email _____

Name _____

Address _____

City, State, Zip Code _____

Phone Nu. _____ Email _____

Name _____

Address _____

City, State, Zip Code _____

Phone Nu. _____ Email _____

Name _____

Address _____

City, State, Zip Code _____

Phone Nu. _____ Email _____

Name _____

Address _____

City, State, Zip Code _____

Phone Nu. _____ Email _____

Name _____

Address _____

City, State, Zip Code _____

Phone Nu. _____ Email _____

Name _____

Address _____

City, State, Zip Code _____

Phone Nu. _____ Email _____

Name _____

Address _____

City, State, Zip Code _____

Phone Nu. _____ Email _____

C

Call your friends

Special notes to remember ......

_____
_____
_____
_____
_____
_____
_____
_____
_____
_____
_____
_____
_____
_____
_____
_____
_____
_____

Name _____

Address _____

City, State, Zip Code _____

Phone Nu. _____ Email _____

Name _____

Address _____

City, State, Zip Code _____

Phone Nu. _____ Email _____

Name _____

Address _____

City, State, Zip Code _____

Phone Nu. _____ Email _____

Name _____

Address _____

City, State, Zip Code _____

Phone Nu. _____ Email _____

Name _____

Address _____

City, State, Zip Code _____

Phone Nu. _____ Email _____

Name _____

Address _____

City, State, Zip Code _____

Phone Nu. _____ Email _____

Name _____

Address _____

City, State, Zip Code _____

Phone Nu. _____ Email _____

Name _____

Address _____

City, State, Zip Code _____

Phone Nu. _____ Email _____

Name _____

Address _____

City, State, Zip Code _____

Phone Nu. _____ Email _____

Name _____

Address _____

City, State, Zip Code _____

Phone Nu. _____ Email _____

Name _____

Address _____

City, State, Zip Code _____

Phone Nu. _____ Email _____

Name _____

Address _____

City, State, Zip Code _____

Phone Nu. _____ Email _____

Name _____

Address _____

City, State, Zip Code _____

Phone Nu. _____ Email _____

Name _____

Address _____

City, State, Zip Code _____

Phone Nu. _____ Email _____

Name _____

Address _____

City, State, Zip Code _____

Phone Nu. _____ Email _____

Name _____

Address _____

City, State, Zip Code _____

Phone Nu. _____ Email _____

D

Don't hold grudges

Special notes to remember ......

_____
_____
_____
_____
_____
_____
_____
_____
_____
_____
_____
_____
_____
_____
_____
_____
_____
_____
_____
_____
_____

Name _____

Address _____

City, State, Zip Code _____

Phone Nu. _____ Email _____

Name _____

Address _____

City, State, Zip Code _____

Phone Nu. _____ Email _____

Name _____

Address _____

City, State, Zip Code _____

Phone Nu. _____ Email _____

Name _____

Address _____

City, State, Zip Code _____

Phone Nu. _____ Email _____

Name _____

Address _____

City, State, Zip Code _____

Phone Nu. _____ Email _____

Name _____

Address _____

City, State, Zip Code _____

Phone Nu. _____ Email _____

Name _____

Address _____

City, State, Zip Code _____

Phone Nu. _____ Email _____

Name _____

Address _____

City, State, Zip Code _____

Phone Nu. _____ Email _____

Name _____
Address _____
City, State, Zip Code _____
Phone Nu. _____ Email _____

Name _____
Address _____
City, State, Zip Code _____
Phone Nu. _____ Email _____

Name _____
Address _____
City, State, Zip Code _____
Phone Nu. _____ Email _____

Name _____
Address _____
City, State, Zip Code _____
Phone Nu. _____ Email _____

Name _____

Address _____

City, State, Zip Code _____

Phone Nu. _____ Email _____

Name _____

Address _____

City, State, Zip Code _____

Phone Nu. _____ Email _____

Name _____

Address _____

City, State, Zip Code _____

Phone Nu. _____ Email _____

Name _____

Address _____

City, State, Zip Code _____

Phone Nu. _____ Email _____

E

Express your love

Special notes to remember ......

_____
_____
_____
_____
_____
_____
_____
_____
_____
_____
_____
_____
_____
_____
_____
_____
_____
_____

Name _____

Address _____

City, State, Zip Code _____

Phone Nu. _____ Email _____

Name _____

Address _____

City, State, Zip Code _____

Phone Nu. _____ Email _____

Name _____

Address _____

City, State, Zip Code _____

Phone Nu. _____ Email _____

Name _____

Address _____

City, State, Zip Code _____

Phone Nu. _____ Email _____

Name _____

Address _____

City, State, Zip Code _____

Phone Nu. _____ Email _____

Name _____

Address _____

City, State, Zip Code _____

Phone Nu. _____ Email _____

Name _____

Address _____

City, State, Zip Code _____

Phone Nu. _____ Email _____

Name _____

Address _____

City, State, Zip Code _____

Phone Nu. _____ Email _____

Name _____

Address _____

City, State, Zip Code _____

Phone Nu. _____ Email _____

Name _____

Address _____

City, State, Zip Code _____

Phone Nu. _____ Email _____

Name _____

Address _____

City, State, Zip Code _____

Phone Nu. _____ Email _____

Name _____

Address _____

City, State, Zip Code _____

Phone Nu. _____ Email _____

Name _____

Address _____

City, State, Zip Code _____

Phone Nu. _____ Email _____

Name _____

Address _____

City, State, Zip Code _____

Phone Nu. _____ Email _____

Name _____

Address _____

City, State, Zip Code _____

Phone Nu. _____ Email _____

Name _____

Address _____

City, State, Zip Code _____

Phone Nu. _____ Email _____

F

Forgive your ememies

Special notes to remember ......

_____
_____
_____
_____
_____
_____
_____
_____
_____
_____
_____
_____
_____
_____
_____
_____

Name _____

Address _____

City, State, Zip Code _____

Phone Nu. _____ Email _____

Name _____

Address _____

City, State, Zip Code _____

Phone Nu. _____ Email _____

Name _____

Address _____

City, State, Zip Code _____

Phone Nu. _____ Email _____

Name _____

Address _____

City, State, Zip Code _____

Phone Nu. _____ Email _____

Name _____

Address _____

City, State, Zip Code _____

Phone Nu. _____ Email _____

Name _____

Address _____

City, State, Zip Code _____

Phone Nu. _____ Email _____

Name _____

Address _____

City, State, Zip Code _____

Phone Nu. _____ Email _____

Name _____

Address _____

City, State, Zip Code _____

Phone Nu. _____ Email _____

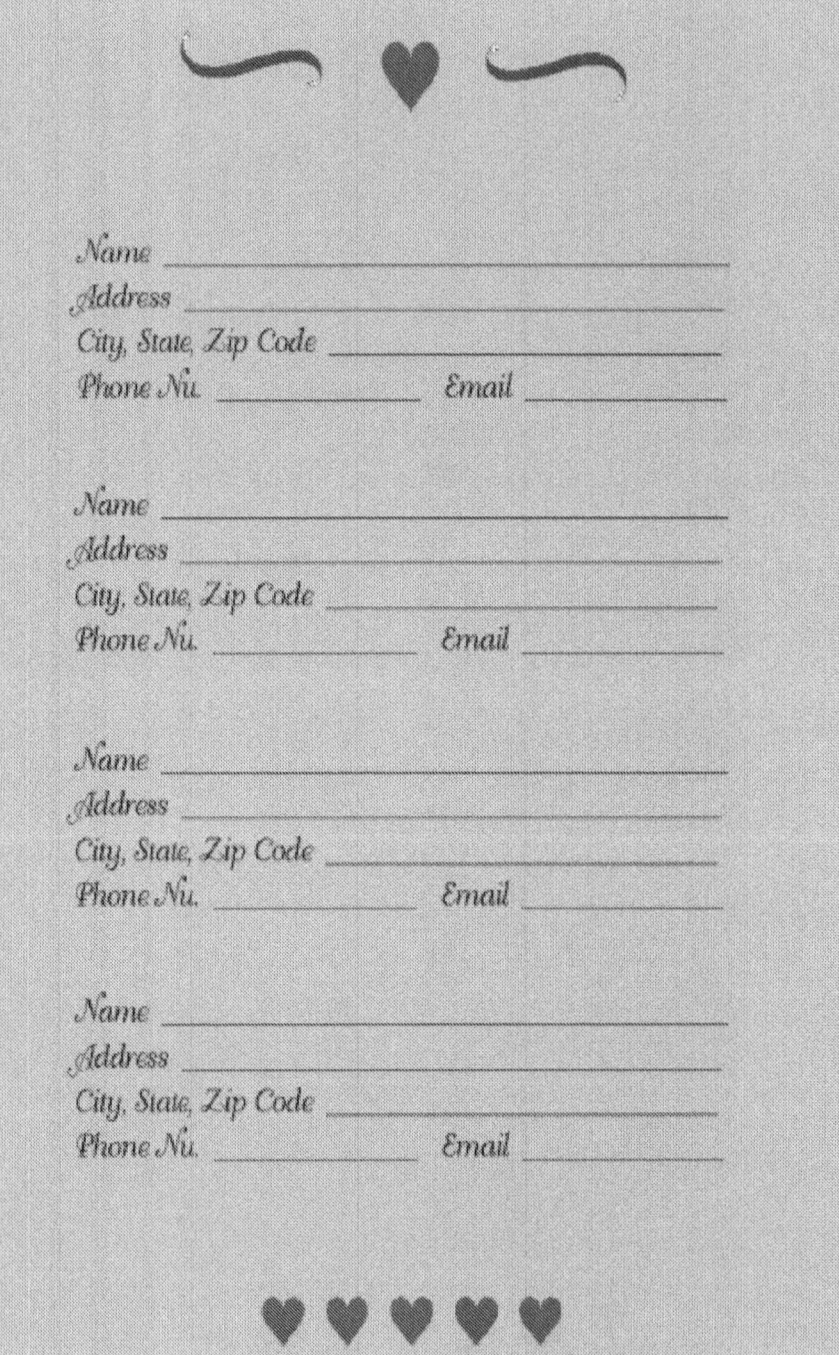

Name _____

Address _____

City, State, Zip Code _____

Phone Nu. _____ Email _____

Name _____

Address _____

City, State, Zip Code _____

Phone Nu. _____ Email _____

Name _____

Address _____

City, State, Zip Code _____

Phone Nu. _____ Email _____

Name _____

Address _____

City, State, Zip Code _____

Phone Nu. _____ Email _____

Name _____

Address _____

City, State, Zip Code _____

Phone Nu. _____ Email _____

Name _____

Address _____

City, State, Zip Code _____

Phone Nu. _____ Email _____

Name _____

Address _____

City, State, Zip Code _____

Phone Nu. _____ Email _____

Name _____

Address _____

City, State, Zip Code _____

Phone Nu. _____ Email _____

G

Give a hug

Special notes to remember ......

_____

_____

_____

_____

_____

_____

_____

_____

_____

_____

_____

_____

_____

_____

_____

_____

_____

_____

Name _____

Address _____

City, State, Zip Code _____

Phone Nu. _____ Email _____

Name _____

Address _____

City, State, Zip Code _____

Phone Nu. _____ Email _____

Name _____

Address _____

City, State, Zip Code _____

Phone Nu. _____ Email _____

Name _____

Address _____

City, State, Zip Code _____

Phone Nu. _____ Email _____

Name _____

Address _____

City, State, Zip Code _____

Phone Nu. _____ Email _____

Name _____

Address _____

City, State, Zip Code _____

Phone Nu. _____ Email _____

Name _____

Address _____

City, State, Zip Code _____

Phone Nu. _____ Email _____

Name _____

Address _____

City, State, Zip Code _____

Phone Nu. _____ Email _____

Name _____

Address _____

City, State, Zip Code _____

Phone Nu. _____ Email _____

Name _____

Address _____

City, State, Zip Code _____

Phone Nu. _____ Email _____

Name _____

Address _____

City, State, Zip Code _____

Phone Nu. _____ Email _____

Name _____

Address _____

City, State, Zip Code _____

Phone Nu. _____ Email _____

Name _____

Address _____

City, State, Zip Code _____

Phone Nu. _____ Email _____

Name _____

Address _____

City, State, Zip Code _____

Phone Nu. _____ Email _____

Name _____

Address _____

City, State, Zip Code _____

Phone Nu. _____ Email _____

Name _____

Address _____

City, State, Zip Code _____

Phone Nu. _____ Email _____

H

Help thy neighbor

Special notes to remember ......

_____
_____
_____
_____
_____
_____
_____
_____
_____
_____
_____
_____
_____
_____
_____
_____
_____
_____
_____

Name _____
Address _____
City, State, Zip Code _____
Phone Nu. _____ Email _____

Name _____
Address _____
City, State, Zip Code _____
Phone Nu. _____ Email _____

Name _____
Address _____
City, State, Zip Code _____
Phone Nu. _____ Email _____

Name _____
Address _____
City, State, Zip Code _____
Phone Nu. _____ Email _____

Name _____

Address _____

City, State, Zip Code _____

Phone Nu. _____ Email _____

Name _____

Address _____

City, State, Zip Code _____

Phone Nu. _____ Email _____

Name _____

Address _____

City, State, Zip Code _____

Phone Nu. _____ Email _____

Name _____

Address _____

City, State, Zip Code _____

Phone Nu. _____ Email _____

Name _____

Address _____

City, State, Zip Code _____

Phone Nu. _____ Email _____

Name _____

Address _____

City, State, Zip Code _____

Phone Nu. _____ Email _____

Name _____

Address _____

City, State, Zip Code _____

Phone Nu. _____ Email _____

Name _____

Address _____

City, State, Zip Code _____

Phone Nu. _____ Email _____

Name _____

Address _____

City, State, Zip Code _____

Phone Nu. _____ Email _____

Name _____

Address _____

City, State, Zip Code _____

Phone Nu. _____ Email _____

Name _____

Address _____

City, State, Zip Code _____

Phone Nu. _____ Email _____

Name _____

Address _____

City, State, Zip Code _____

Phone Nu. _____ Email _____

I

Interact with people

Special notes to remember ......

_____

_____

_____

_____

_____

_____

_____

_____

_____

_____

_____

_____

_____

_____

_____

_____

_____

_____

Name _____

Address _____

City, State, Zip Code _____

Phone Nu. _____ Email _____

Name _____

Address _____

City, State, Zip Code _____

Phone Nu. _____ Email _____

Name _____

Address _____

City, State, Zip Code _____

Phone Nu. _____ Email _____

Name _____

Address _____

City, State, Zip Code _____

Phone Nu. _____ Email _____

Name _____

Address _____

City, State, Zip Code _____

Phone Nu. _____ Email _____

Name _____

Address _____

City, State, Zip Code _____

Phone Nu. _____ Email _____

Name _____

Address _____

City, State, Zip Code _____

Phone Nu. _____ Email _____

Name _____

Address _____

City, State, Zip Code _____

Phone Nu. _____ Email _____

Name _____

Address _____

City, State, Zip Code _____

Phone Nu. _____ Email _____

Name _____

Address _____

City, State, Zip Code _____

Phone Nu. _____ Email _____

Name _____

Address _____

City, State, Zip Code _____

Phone Nu. _____ Email _____

Name _____

Address _____

City, State, Zip Code _____

Phone Nu. _____ Email _____

Name _____
Address _____
City, State, Zip Code _____
Phone Nu. _____ Email _____

Name _____
Address _____
City, State, Zip Code _____
Phone Nu. _____ Email _____

Name _____
Address _____
City, State, Zip Code _____
Phone Nu. _____ Email _____

Name _____
Address _____
City, State, Zip Code _____
Phone Nu. _____ Email _____

J

Join a club

Special notes to remember ......

_____
_____
_____
_____
_____
_____
_____
_____
_____
_____
_____
_____
_____
_____
_____
_____
_____
_____
_____
_____
_____

Name _____
Address _____
City, State, Zip Code _____
Phone Nu. _____ Email _____

Name _____
Address _____
City, State, Zip Code _____
Phone Nu. _____ Email _____

Name _____
Address _____
City, State, Zip Code _____
Phone Nu. _____ Email _____

Name _____
Address _____
City, State, Zip Code _____
Phone Nu. _____ Email _____

Name _____
Address _____
City, State, Zip Code _____
Phone Nu. _____ Email _____

Name _____
Address _____
City, State, Zip Code _____
Phone Nu. _____ Email _____

Name _____
Address _____
City, State, Zip Code _____
Phone Nu. _____ Email _____

Name _____
Address _____
City, State, Zip Code _____
Phone Nu. _____ Email _____

Name _____

Address _____

City, State, Zip Code _____

Phone Nu. _____ Email _____

Name _____

Address _____

City, State, Zip Code _____

Phone Nu. _____ Email _____

Name _____

Address _____

City, State, Zip Code _____

Phone Nu. _____ Email _____

Name _____

Address _____

City, State, Zip Code _____

Phone Nu. _____ Email _____

Name _____

Address _____

City, State, Zip Code _____

Phone Nu. _____ Email _____

Name _____

Address _____

City, State, Zip Code _____

Phone Nu. _____ Email _____

Name _____

Address _____

City, State, Zip Code _____

Phone Nu. _____ Email _____

Name _____

Address _____

City, State, Zip Code _____

Phone Nu. _____ Email _____

Special notes to remember ......

_____
_____
_____
_____
_____
_____
_____
_____
_____
_____
_____
_____
_____
_____
_____
_____
_____

Name _____

Address _____

City, State, Zip Code _____

Phone Nu. _____ Email _____

Name _____

Address _____

City, State, Zip Code _____

Phone Nu. _____ Email _____

Name _____

Address _____

City, State, Zip Code _____

Phone Nu. _____ Email _____

Name _____

Address _____

City, State, Zip Code _____

Phone Nu. _____ Email _____

Name _____

Address _____

City, State, Zip Code _____

Phone Nu. _____ Email _____

Name _____

Address _____

City, State, Zip Code _____

Phone Nu. _____ Email _____

Name _____

Address _____

City, State, Zip Code _____

Phone Nu. _____ Email _____

Name _____

Address _____

City, State, Zip Code _____

Phone Nu. _____ Email _____

Name _____

Address _____

City, State, Zip Code _____

Phone Nu. _____ Email _____

Name _____

Address _____

City, State, Zip Code _____

Phone Nu. _____ Email _____

Name _____

Address _____

City, State, Zip Code _____

Phone Nu. _____ Email _____

Name _____

Address _____

City, State, Zip Code _____

Phone Nu. _____ Email _____

Name _____
Address _____
City, State, Zip Code _____
Phone Nu. _____ Email _____

Name _____
Address _____
City, State, Zip Code _____
Phone Nu. _____ Email _____

Name _____
Address _____
City, State, Zip Code _____
Phone Nu. _____ Email _____

Name _____
Address _____
City, State, Zip Code _____
Phone Nu. _____ Email _____

L

Love thy neighbor

Special notes to remember ......

_____

_____

_____

_____

_____

_____

_____

_____

_____

_____

_____

_____

_____

_____

_____

_____

_____

♥ ♥ ♥ ♥ ♥

Name _____

Address _____

City, State, Zip Code _____

Phone Nu. _____ Email _____

Name _____

Address _____

City, State, Zip Code _____

Phone Nu. _____ Email _____

Name _____

Address _____

City, State, Zip Code _____

Phone Nu. _____ Email _____

Name _____

Address _____

City, State, Zip Code _____

Phone Nu. _____ Email _____

Name _____

Address _____

City, State, Zip Code _____

Phone Nu. _____ Email _____

Name _____

Address _____

City, State, Zip Code _____

Phone Nu. _____ Email _____

Name _____

Address _____

City, State, Zip Code _____

Phone Nu. _____ Email _____

Name _____

Address _____

City, State, Zip Code _____

Phone Nu. _____ Email _____

Name _____

Address _____

City, State, Zip Code _____

Phone Nu. _____ Email _____

Name _____

Address _____

City, State, Zip Code _____

Phone Nu. _____ Email _____

Name _____

Address _____

City, State, Zip Code _____

Phone Nu. _____ Email _____

Name _____

Address _____

City, State, Zip Code _____

Phone Nu. _____ Email _____

Name _____

Address _____

City, State, Zip Code _____

Phone Nu. _____ Email _____

Name _____

Address _____

City, State, Zip Code _____

Phone Nu. _____ Email _____

Name _____

Address _____

City, State, Zip Code _____

Phone Nu. _____ Email _____

Name _____

Address _____

City, State, Zip Code _____

Phone Nu. _____ Email _____

M

Make a friend

Special notes to remember ......

_____

_____

_____

_____

_____

_____

_____

_____

_____

_____

_____

_____

_____

_____

_____

_____

_____

_____

Name _____

Address _____

City, State, Zip Code _____

Phone Nu. _____ Email _____

Name _____

Address _____

City, State, Zip Code _____

Phone Nu. _____ Email _____

Name _____

Address _____

City, State, Zip Code _____

Phone Nu. _____ Email _____

Name _____

Address _____

City, State, Zip Code _____

Phone Nu. _____ Email _____

Name _____

Address _____

City, State, Zip Code _____

Phone Nu. _____ Email _____

Name _____

Address _____

City, State, Zip Code _____

Phone Nu. _____ Email _____

Name _____

Address _____

City, State, Zip Code _____

Phone Nu. _____ Email _____

Name _____

Address _____

City, State, Zip Code _____

Phone Nu. _____ Email _____

Name _____

Address _____

City, State, Zip Code _____

Phone Nu. _____ Email _____

Name _____

Address _____

City, State, Zip Code _____

Phone Nu. _____ Email _____

Name _____

Address _____

City, State, Zip Code _____

Phone Nu. _____ Email _____

Name _____

Address _____

City, State, Zip Code _____

Phone Nu. _____ Email _____

Name _____

Address _____

City, State, Zip Code _____

Phone Nu. _____ Email _____

Name _____

Address _____

City, State, Zip Code _____

Phone Nu. _____ Email _____

Name _____

Address _____

City, State, Zip Code _____

Phone Nu. _____ Email _____

Name _____

Address _____

City, State, Zip Code _____

Phone Nu. _____ Email _____

N

Never insult anyone

Special notes to remember ......

_____
_____
_____
_____
_____
_____
_____
_____
_____
_____
_____
_____
_____
_____
_____
_____
_____
_____

Name _____

Address _____

City, State, Zip Code _____

Phone Nu. _____ Email _____

Name _____

Address _____

City, State, Zip Code _____

Phone Nu. _____ Email _____

Name _____

Address _____

City, State, Zip Code _____

Phone Nu. _____ Email _____

Name _____

Address _____

City, State, Zip Code _____

Phone Nu. _____ Email _____

Name _____

Address _____

City, State, Zip Code _____

Phone Nu. _____ Email _____

Name _____

Address _____

City, State, Zip Code _____

Phone Nu. _____ Email _____

Name _____

Address _____

City, State, Zip Code _____

Phone Nu. _____ Email _____

Name _____

Address _____

City, State, Zip Code _____

Phone Nu. _____ Email _____

Name _____

Address _____

City, State, Zip Code _____

Phone Nu. _____ Email _____

Name _____

Address _____

City, State, Zip Code _____

Phone Nu. _____ Email _____

Name _____

Address _____

City, State, Zip Code _____

Phone Nu. _____ Email _____

Name _____

Address _____

City, State, Zip Code _____

Phone Nu. _____ Email _____

Name _____

Address _____

City, State, Zip Code _____

Phone Nu. _____ Email _____

Name _____

Address _____

City, State, Zip Code _____

Phone Nu. _____ Email _____

Name _____

Address _____

City, State, Zip Code _____

Phone Nu. _____ Email _____

Name _____

Address _____

City, State, Zip Code _____

Phone Nu. _____ Email _____

O

Open your heart

Special notes to remember ......

_____

_____

_____

_____

_____

_____

_____

_____

_____

_____

_____

_____

_____

_____

_____

_____

_____

_____

_____

_____

♥ ♥ ♥ ♥ ♥

Name _____

Address _____

City, State, Zip Code _____

Phone Nu. _____ Email _____

Name _____

Address _____

City, State, Zip Code _____

Phone Nu. _____ Email _____

Name _____

Address _____

City, State, Zip Code _____

Phone Nu. _____ Email _____

Name _____

Address _____

City, State, Zip Code _____

Phone Nu. _____ Email _____

Name _____

Address _____

City, State, Zip Code _____

Phone Nu. _____ Email _____

Name _____

Address _____

City, State, Zip Code _____

Phone Nu. _____ Email _____

Name _____

Address _____

City, State, Zip Code _____

Phone Nu. _____ Email _____

Name _____

Address _____

City, State, Zip Code _____

Phone Nu. _____ Email _____

Name _____

Address _____

City, State, Zip Code _____

Phone Nu. _____ Email _____

Name _____

Address _____

City, State, Zip Code _____

Phone Nu. _____ Email _____

Name _____

Address _____

City, State, Zip Code _____

Phone Nu. _____ Email _____

Name _____

Address _____

City, State, Zip Code _____

Phone Nu. _____ Email _____

Name _____

Address _____

City, State, Zip Code _____

Phone Nu. _____ Email _____

Name _____

Address _____

City, State, Zip Code _____

Phone Nu. _____ Email _____

Name _____

Address _____

City, State, Zip Code _____

Phone Nu. _____ Email _____

Name _____

Address _____

City, State, Zip Code _____

Phone Nu. _____ Email _____

P

Pray for America

Special notes to remember ......

_____

_____

_____

_____

_____

_____

_____

_____

_____

_____

_____

_____

_____

_____

_____

_____

_____

Name _____
Address _____
City, State, Zip Code _____
Phone Nu. _____ Email _____

Name _____
Address _____
City, State, Zip Code _____
Phone Nu. _____ Email _____

Name _____
Address _____
City, State, Zip Code _____
Phone Nu. _____ Email _____

Name _____
Address _____
City, State, Zip Code _____
Phone Nu. _____ Email _____

Name _____
Address _____
City, State, Zip Code _____
Phone Nu. _____ Email _____

Name _____
Address _____
City, State, Zip Code _____
Phone Nu. _____ Email _____

Name _____
Address _____
City, State, Zip Code _____
Phone Nu. _____ Email _____

Name _____
Address _____
City, State, Zip Code _____
Phone Nu. _____ Email _____

Name _____

Address _____

City, State, Zip Code _____

Phone Nu. _____ Email _____

Name _____

Address _____

City, State, Zip Code _____

Phone Nu. _____ Email _____

Name _____

Address _____

City, State, Zip Code _____

Phone Nu. _____ Email _____

Name _____

Address _____

City, State, Zip Code _____

Phone Nu. _____ Email _____

Name _____

Address _____

City, State, Zip Code _____

Phone Nu. _____ Email _____

Name _____

Address _____

City, State, Zip Code _____

Phone Nu. _____ Email _____

Name _____

Address _____

City, State, Zip Code _____

Phone Nu. _____ Email _____

Name _____

Address _____

City, State, Zip Code _____

Phone Nu. _____ Email _____

Q

Quiet time together

Special notes to remember ......

_____
_____
_____
_____
_____
_____
_____
_____
_____
_____
_____
_____
_____
_____
_____
_____
_____
_____

Name _____

Address _____

City, State, Zip Code _____

Phone Nu. _____ Email _____

Name _____

Address _____

City, State, Zip Code _____

Phone Nu. _____ Email _____

Name _____

Address _____

City, State, Zip Code _____

Phone Nu. _____ Email _____

Name _____

Address _____

City, State, Zip Code _____

Phone Nu. _____ Email _____

Name _____

Address _____

City, State, Zip Code _____

Phone Nu. _____ Email _____

Name _____

Address _____

City, State, Zip Code _____

Phone Nu. _____ Email _____

Name _____

Address _____

City, State, Zip Code _____

Phone Nu. _____ Email _____

Name _____

Address _____

City, State, Zip Code _____

Phone Nu. _____ Email _____

Name _____
Address _____
City, State, Zip Code _____
Phone Nu. _____ Email _____

Name _____
Address _____
City, State, Zip Code _____
Phone Nu. _____ Email _____

Name _____
Address _____
City, State, Zip Code _____
Phone Nu. _____ Email _____

Name _____
Address _____
City, State, Zip Code _____
Phone Nu. _____ Email _____

Name _____

Address _____

City, State, Zip Code _____

Phone Nu. _____ Email _____

Name _____

Address _____

City, State, Zip Code _____

Phone Nu. _____ Email _____

Name _____

Address _____

City, State, Zip Code _____

Phone Nu. _____ Email _____

Name _____

Address _____

City, State, Zip Code _____

Phone Nu. _____ Email _____

R

Remember your friends

Special notes to remember ......

_____

_____

_____

_____

_____

_____

_____

_____

_____

_____

_____

_____

_____

_____

_____

_____

_____

_____

_____

♥ ♥ ♥ ♥ ♥

Name _____

Address _____

City, State, Zip Code _____

Phone Nu. _____ Email _____

Name _____

Address _____

City, State, Zip Code _____

Phone Nu. _____ Email _____

Name _____

Address _____

City, State, Zip Code _____

Phone Nu. _____ Email _____

Name _____

Address _____

City, State, Zip Code _____

Phone Nu. _____ Email _____

Name _____
Address _____
City, State, Zip Code _____
Phone Nu. _____ Email _____

Name _____
Address _____
City, State, Zip Code _____
Phone Nu. _____ Email _____

Name _____
Address _____
City, State, Zip Code _____
Phone Nu. _____ Email _____

Name _____
Address _____
City, State, Zip Code _____
Phone Nu. _____ Email _____

Name _____

Address _____

City, State, Zip Code _____

Phone Nu. _____ Email _____

Name _____

Address _____

City, State, Zip Code _____

Phone Nu. _____ Email _____

Name _____

Address _____

City, State, Zip Code _____

Phone Nu. _____ Email _____

Name _____

Address _____

City, State, Zip Code _____

Phone Nu. _____ Email _____

Name _____

Address _____

City, State, Zip Code _____

Phone Nu. _____ Email _____

Name _____

Address _____

City, State, Zip Code _____

Phone Nu. _____ Email _____

Name _____

Address _____

City, State, Zip Code _____

Phone Nu. _____ Email _____

Name _____

Address _____

City, State, Zip Code _____

Phone Nu. _____ Email _____

S

Share a story

Special notes to remember ......

Name _____

Address _____

City, State, Zip Code _____

Phone Nu. _____ Email _____

Name _____

Address _____

City, State, Zip Code _____

Phone Nu. _____ Email _____

Name _____

Address _____

City, State, Zip Code _____

Phone Nu. _____ Email _____

Name _____

Address _____

City, State, Zip Code _____

Phone Nu. _____ Email _____

Name _____

Address _____

City, State, Zip Code _____

Phone Nu. _____ Email _____

Name _____

Address _____

City, State, Zip Code _____

Phone Nu. _____ Email _____

Name _____

Address _____

City, State, Zip Code _____

Phone Nu. _____ Email _____

Name _____

Address _____

City, State, Zip Code _____

Phone Nu. _____ Email _____

Name _____

Address _____

City, State, Zip Code _____

Phone Nu. _____ Email _____

Name _____

Address _____

City, State, Zip Code _____

Phone Nu. _____ Email _____

Name _____

Address _____

City, State, Zip Code _____

Phone Nu. _____ Email _____

Name _____

Address _____

City, State, Zip Code _____

Phone Nu. _____ Email _____

Name _____

Address _____

City, State, Zip Code _____

Phone Nu. _____ Email _____

Name _____

Address _____

City, State, Zip Code _____

Phone Nu. _____ Email _____

Name _____

Address _____

City, State, Zip Code _____

Phone Nu. _____ Email _____

Name _____

Address _____

City, State, Zip Code _____

Phone Nu. _____ Email _____

T

Take time out

Special notes to remember ......

_____

_____

_____

_____

_____

_____

_____

_____

_____

_____

_____

_____

_____

_____

_____

_____

_____

Name _____
Address _____
City, State, Zip Code _____
Phone Nu. _____ Email _____

Name _____
Address _____
City, State, Zip Code _____
Phone Nu. _____ Email _____

Name _____
Address _____
City, State, Zip Code _____
Phone Nu. _____ Email _____

Name _____
Address _____
City, State, Zip Code _____
Phone Nu. _____ Email _____

Name _____

Address _____

City, State, Zip Code _____

Phone Nu. _____ Email _____

Name _____

Address _____

City, State, Zip Code _____

Phone Nu. _____ Email _____

Name _____

Address _____

City, State, Zip Code _____

Phone Nu. _____ Email _____

Name _____

Address _____

City, State, Zip Code _____

Phone Nu. _____ Email _____

Name _____

Address _____

City, State, Zip Code _____

Phone Nu. _____ Email _____

Name _____

Address _____

City, State, Zip Code _____

Phone Nu. _____ Email _____

Name _____

Address _____

City, State, Zip Code _____

Phone Nu. _____ Email _____

Name _____

Address _____

City, State, Zip Code _____

Phone Nu. _____ Email _____

Name _____

Address _____

City, State, Zip Code _____

Phone Nu. _____ Email _____

Name _____

Address _____

City, State, Zip Code _____

Phone Nu. _____ Email _____

Name _____

Address _____

City, State, Zip Code _____

Phone Nu. _____ Email _____

Name _____

Address _____

City, State, Zip Code _____

Phone Nu. _____ Email _____

U

Uphold your promises

Special notes to remember ......

_____
_____
_____
_____
_____
_____
_____
_____
_____
_____
_____
_____
_____
_____
_____
_____
_____

Name _____

Address _____

City, State, Zip Code _____

Phone Nu. _____ Email _____

Name _____

Address _____

City, State, Zip Code _____

Phone Nu. _____ Email _____

Name _____

Address _____

City, State, Zip Code _____

Phone Nu. _____ Email _____

Name _____

Address _____

City, State, Zip Code _____

Phone Nu. _____ Email _____

Name _____

Address _____

City, State, Zip Code _____

Phone Nu. _____ Email _____

Name _____

Address _____

City, State, Zip Code _____

Phone Nu. _____ Email _____

Name _____

Address _____

City, State, Zip Code _____

Phone Nu. _____ Email _____

Name _____

Address _____

City, State, Zip Code _____

Phone Nu. _____ Email _____

Name _____

Address _____

City, State, Zip Code _____

Phone Nu. _____ Email _____

Name _____

Address _____

City, State, Zip Code _____

Phone Nu. _____ Email _____

Name _____

Address _____

City, State, Zip Code _____

Phone Nu. _____ Email _____

Name _____

Address _____

City, State, Zip Code _____

Phone Nu. _____ Email _____

Name _____

Address _____

City, State, Zip Code _____

Phone Nu. _____ Email _____

Name _____

Address _____

City, State, Zip Code _____

Phone Nu. _____ Email _____

Name _____

Address _____

City, State, Zip Code _____

Phone Nu. _____ Email _____

Name _____

Address _____

City, State, Zip Code _____

Phone Nu. _____ Email _____

V

Visit a friend

Special notes to remember ......

_____
_____
_____
_____
_____
_____
_____
_____
_____
_____
_____
_____
_____
_____
_____
_____
_____
_____

Name _____

Address _____

City, State, Zip Code _____

Phone Nu. _____ Email _____

Name _____

Address _____

City, State, Zip Code _____

Phone Nu. _____ Email _____

Name _____

Address _____

City, State, Zip Code _____

Phone Nu. _____ Email _____

Name _____

Address _____

City, State, Zip Code _____

Phone Nu. _____ Email _____

Name _____

Address _____

City, State, Zip Code _____

Phone Nu. _____ Email _____

Name _____

Address _____

City, State, Zip Code _____

Phone Nu. _____ Email _____

Name _____

Address _____

City, State, Zip Code _____

Phone Nu. _____ Email _____

Name _____

Address _____

City, State, Zip Code _____

Phone Nu. _____ Email _____

Name _____

Address _____

City, State, Zip Code _____

Phone Nu. _____ Email _____

Name _____

Address _____

City, State, Zip Code _____

Phone Nu. _____ Email _____

Name _____

Address _____

City, State, Zip Code _____

Phone Nu. _____ Email _____

Name _____

Address _____

City, State, Zip Code _____

Phone Nu. _____ Email _____

Name _____

Address _____

City, State, Zip Code _____

Phone Nu. _____ Email _____

Name _____

Address _____

City, State, Zip Code _____

Phone Nu. _____ Email _____

Name _____

Address _____

City, State, Zip Code _____

Phone Nu. _____ Email _____

Name _____

Address _____

City, State, Zip Code _____

Phone Nu. _____ Email _____

W

Write a letter

Special notes to remember ......

_____
_____
_____
_____
_____
_____
_____
_____
_____
_____
_____
_____
_____
_____
_____
_____
_____

Name _____

Address _____

City, State, Zip Code _____

Phone Nu. _____ Email _____

Name _____

Address _____

City, State, Zip Code _____

Phone Nu. _____ Email _____

Name _____

Address _____

City, State, Zip Code _____

Phone Nu. _____ Email _____

Name _____

Address _____

City, State, Zip Code _____

Phone Nu. _____ Email _____

Name _____

Address _____

City, State, Zip Code _____

Phone Nu. _____ Email _____

Name _____

Address _____

City, State, Zip Code _____

Phone Nu. _____ Email _____

Name _____

Address _____

City, State, Zip Code _____

Phone Nu. _____ Email _____

Name _____

Address _____

City, State, Zip Code _____

Phone Nu. _____ Email _____

Name _____

Address _____

City, State, Zip Code _____

Phone Nu. _____ Email _____

Name _____

Address _____

City, State, Zip Code _____

Phone Nu. _____ Email _____

Name _____

Address _____

City, State, Zip Code _____

Phone Nu. _____ Email _____

Name _____

Address _____

City, State, Zip Code _____

Phone Nu. _____ Email _____

Name _____

Address _____

City, State, Zip Code _____

Phone Nu. _____ Email _____

Name _____

Address _____

City, State, Zip Code _____

Phone Nu. _____ Email _____

Name _____

Address _____

City, State, Zip Code _____

Phone Nu. _____ Email _____

Name _____

Address _____

City, State, Zip Code _____

Phone Nu. _____ Email _____

X

Xerox your poems

Special notes to remember ......

_____

_____

_____

_____

_____

_____

_____

_____

_____

_____

_____

_____

_____

_____

_____

_____

♥ ♥ ♥ ♥ ♥

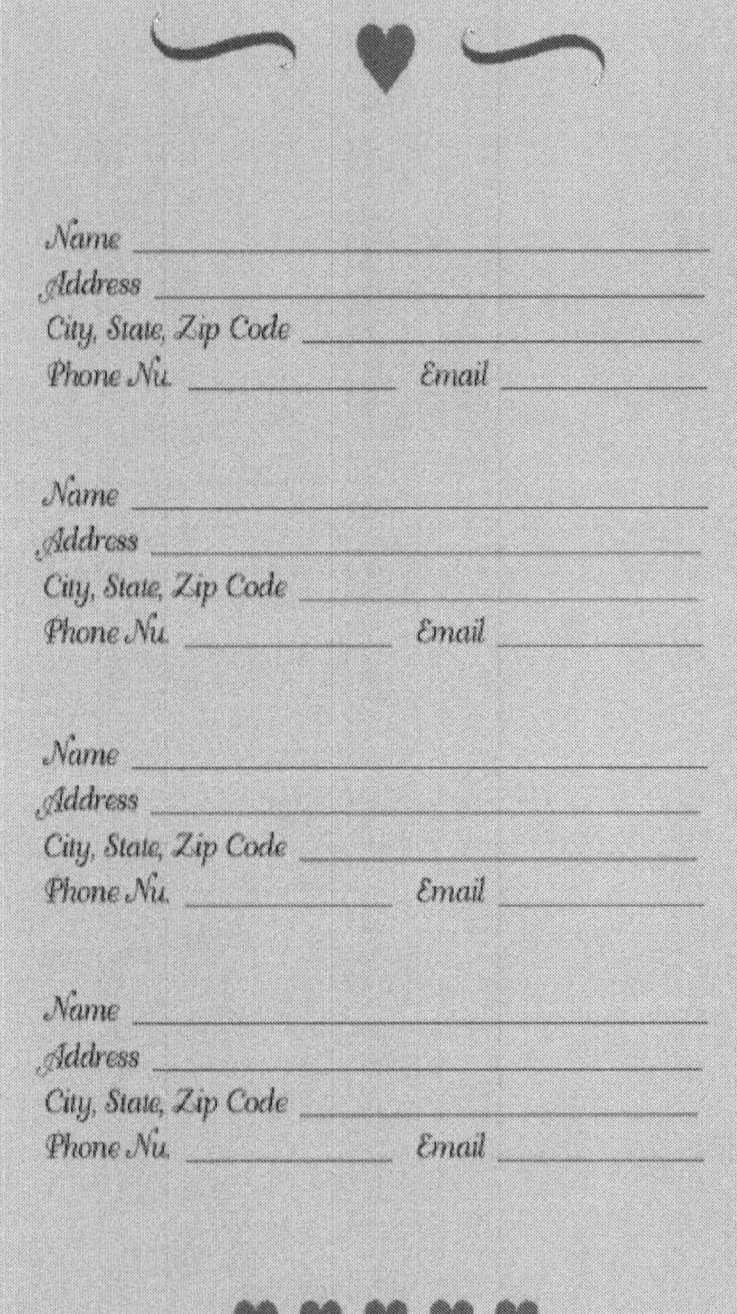

Name _____

Address _____

City, State, Zip Code _____

Phone Nu. _____ Email _____

Name _____

Address _____

City, State, Zip Code _____

Phone Nu. _____ Email _____

Name _____

Address _____

City, State, Zip Code _____

Phone Nu. _____ Email _____

Name _____

Address _____

City, State, Zip Code _____

Phone Nu. _____ Email _____

Name _____

Address _____

City, State, Zip Code _____

Phone Nu. _____ Email _____

Name _____

Address _____

City, State, Zip Code _____

Phone Nu. _____ Email _____

Name _____

Address _____

City, State, Zip Code _____

Phone Nu. _____ Email _____

Name _____

Address _____

City, State, Zip Code _____

Phone Nu. _____ Email _____

Name _____

Address _____

City, State, Zip Code _____

Phone Nu. _____ Email _____

Name _____

Address _____

City, State, Zip Code _____

Phone Nu. _____ Email _____

Name _____

Address _____

City, State, Zip Code _____

Phone Nu. _____ Email _____

Name _____

Address _____

City, State, Zip Code _____

Phone Nu. _____ Email _____

Name _____

Address _____

City, State, Zip Code _____

Phone Nu. _____ Email _____

Name _____

Address _____

City, State, Zip Code _____

Phone Nu. _____ Email _____

Name _____

Address _____

City, State, Zip Code _____

Phone Nu. _____ Email _____

Name _____

Address _____

City, State, Zip Code _____

Phone Nu. _____ Email _____

Y

Yearn for love

Special notes to remember ......

Name _____

Address _____

City, State, Zip Code _____

Phone Nu. _____ Email _____

Name _____

Address _____

City, State, Zip Code _____

Phone Nu. _____ Email _____

Name _____

Address _____

City, State, Zip Code _____

Phone Nu. _____ Email _____

Name _____

Address _____

City, State, Zip Code _____

Phone Nu. _____ Email _____

Name _____

Address _____

City, State, Zip Code _____

Phone Nu. _____ Email _____

Name _____

Address _____

City, State, Zip Code _____

Phone Nu. _____ Email _____

Name _____

Address _____

City, State, Zip Code _____

Phone Nu. _____ Email _____

Name _____

Address _____

City, State, Zip Code _____

Phone Nu. _____ Email _____

Name _____
Address _____
City, State, Zip Code _____
Phone Nu. _____ Email _____

Name _____
Address _____
City, State, Zip Code _____
Phone Nu. _____ Email _____

Name _____
Address _____
City, State, Zip Code _____
Phone Nu. _____ Email _____

Name _____
Address _____
City, State, Zip Code _____
Phone Nu. _____ Email _____

Name _____
Address _____
City, State, Zip Code _____
Phone Nu. _____ Email _____

Name _____
Address _____
City, State, Zip Code _____
Phone Nu. _____ Email _____

Name _____
Address _____
City, State, Zip Code _____
Phone Nu. _____ Email _____

Name _____
Address _____
City, State, Zip Code _____
Phone Nu. _____ Email _____

Z

Zoom in relationships

Special notes to remember ......

_____
_____
_____
_____
_____
_____
_____
_____
_____
_____
_____
_____
_____
_____
_____
_____
_____
_____

Name _____
Address _____
City, State, Zip Code _____
Phone Nu. _____ Email _____

Name _____
Address _____
City, State, Zip Code _____
Phone Nu. _____ Email _____

Name _____
Address _____
City, State, Zip Code _____
Phone Nu. _____ Email _____

Name _____
Address _____
City, State, Zip Code _____
Phone Nu. _____ Email _____

Name _____
Address _____
City, State, Zip Code _____
Phone Nu. _____ Email _____

Name _____
Address _____
City, State, Zip Code _____
Phone Nu. _____ Email _____

Name _____
Address _____
City, State, Zip Code _____
Phone Nu. _____ Email _____

Name _____
Address _____
City, State, Zip Code _____
Phone Nu. _____ Email _____

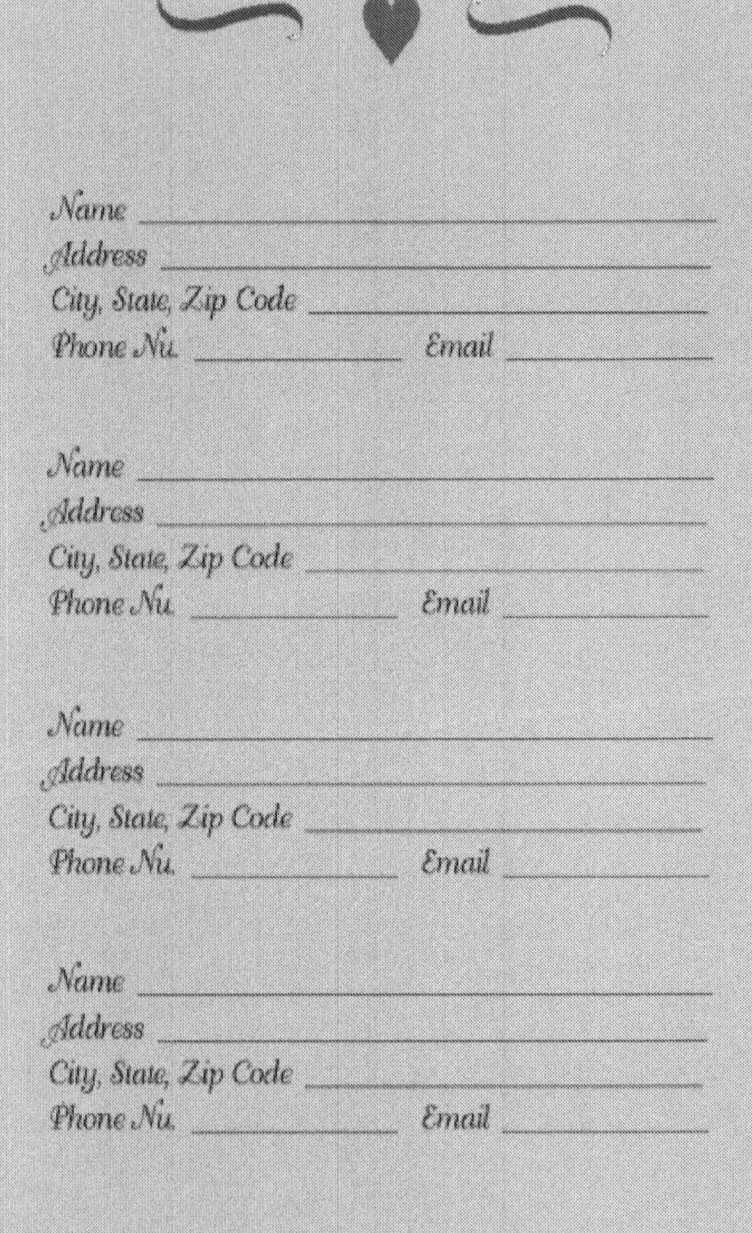

Name _____

Address _____

City, State, Zip Code _____

Phone Nu. _____ Email _____

Name _____

Address _____

City, State, Zip Code _____

Phone Nu. _____ Email _____

Name _____

Address _____

City, State, Zip Code _____

Phone Nu. _____ Email _____

Name _____

Address _____

City, State, Zip Code _____

Phone Nu. _____ Email _____

Name _____

Address _____

City, State, Zip Code _____

Phone Nu. _____ Email _____

Name _____

Address _____

City, State, Zip Code _____

Phone Nu. _____ Email _____

Name _____

Address _____

City, State, Zip Code _____

Phone Nu. _____ Email _____

Name _____

Address _____

City, State, Zip Code _____

Phone Nu. _____ Email _____

About the Author

My name is Linda Blair. I have 3 wonderful children named Hannah, Henry, and Adam; I also have a wonderful husband named Ron. They are the love of my life next to my families and friends.

I believe that keeping in touch with loved ones is very important in life because with them life is much happier and worth living – am I right?

When I thought of doing a book, I wanted it to be something simple rather than something complicated so I came up with this idea of doing an address & phone number book so I hope you find this book will come in handy for you and your family.